CASTLES & FORTS OF GHANA

with the kind support of

CASTLES & FORTS OF GHANA

KWESI J. ANQUANDAH

Christiansborg Castle, Accra - Fort Good Hope, Senya Beraku
Fort Patience, Apam - Fort Amsterdam (Cormantin), Abandze
Fort William, Anomabu - Cape Coast Castle, Cape Coast
Castle St. Jorge, Elmina - Fort St. Jago, Elmina
Fort St. Sebastian, Shama - Fort Orange, Sekondi - Fort Batenstein, Butre
Fort Metal Cross, Dixcove - Gross-Friedrichsburg, Princestown
Fort St. Anthony, Axim - Fort Apollonia, Beyin

GHANA MUSEUMS & MONUMENTS BOARD
ATALANTE

CONTENTS

INTRODUCTION

HISTORY : Castles and Forts in History **P. 8**   **ARCHITECTURE** : Nature, Types, Functions **P. 10**
INSIDE THE FORT : Life and Organization **P. 12**   **OUTSIDE THE FORT** : African-European Relations and Impact **P. 14**
GEOGRAPHY : Distribution and Chronology **P. 20**

CASTLES AND FORTS

CHRISTIANSBORG CASTLE Accra **P.24**   **FORT GOOD HOPE** Senya Beraku **P.30**
FORT PATIENCE Apam **P.34**   **FORT AMSTERDAM (CORMANTIN)** Abandze **P.38**
FORT WILLIAM Anomabu **P.42**   **CAPE COAST CASTLE** Cape Coast **P.46**
ELMINA CASTLE Elmina **P.52**   **FORT ST. JAGO (COENRAADSBURG)** Elmina **P.62**
FORT ST. SEBASTIAN Shama **P.64**   **FORT ORANGE** Sekondi **P.70**
FORT BATENSTEIN Butre **P.74**   **FORT METAL CROSS** Dixcove **P.78**
GROSS-FRIEDRICHSBURG Princestown **P.84**   **FORT ST. ANTHONY** Axim **P.90**
FORT APOLLONIA Beyin **P.96**

CONCLUSION

THE GATES OF RETURN p. 102
ANNEX p. 108

Previous page : Shama, where gold was traded for
the first time (1471) by the Portuguese.

INTRODUCTION

History : Castles and Forts in History
Architecture : Nature, Types, Functions
Inside the Fort : Life and Organization
Outside the Fort : African-European Relations and Impact
Geography : Distribution and Chronology

HISTORY

CASTLES AND FORTS IN HISTORY

The castles and forts of Ghana constitute treasures par excellence, a legacy of the historic past as much to modern Ghana and Africa as to the world at large. Though built on African soil, their authors came from Europe - Portuguese, Dutch, French, Britons, Brandenburg-Prussians, Danes and Swedes. For several centuries, European masters and native African servants lived and worked in them. The warehouses teemed with gold and ivory export products as well as African slaves destined for auction in the New World, there to become ancestors to future generations of black populations. Indeed, these historic buildings were no respectors of persons and extraordinary history was made once when one castle, Elmina, held prisoner an Asante King in all his splendour during the first stage of his forced exile from Ghana. Hence, not only modern Ghanaians, but also many millions in countries of the Western hemisphere and elsewhere constitute stake-holders with an interest in ensuring the preservation of these historic castles and forts.

Recognizing their unique place in world history, the World Heritage Convention of UNESCO has designated Ghana's castles and forts as World Heritage Monuments. (The Convention's philosophy is that "there are some parts of heritage which are of such outstanding value to the world as a whole that their protection, conservation and transmission to future generations is a matter not just for any one nation but for the international community as a whole". (*Monumentum International Journal*, 1984).

Pioneers of Mina

The origins of Ghana's historic fortification system are associated with the epoch-making saga of 15th century Portuguese exploration in Africa, sponsored by the Royal House of Portugal. Henry the Navigator, son of King John I, had a broad vision of exploring Africa's coasts, locating and gaining direct access to the sources of the West African gold trade, circumnavigating Africa, expanding Christendom through evangelism and reaching out to the East Indies to capture the lucrative Asian trade for Europe.

Assisted by elite geographers, cartographers, astronomers and mariners, Portuguese explorers chartered the seas beyond the Canaries and Cape Bojador. In 1471, Martim Fernandes and Alvaro Esteves "discovered" the rich gold lands straddling the valleys of the Ankobra and Volta Rivers. A delighted King Afonso V named the region *Mina*, The Mine, and somewhere around Shama, the Portuguese initiated their barter in gold with the natives. King John II commissioned Diego d'Azambuja to undertake the task of constructing a fortress at the twin-village of Edina in 1482 with the assistance of 600 men including masons, carpenters, engineers, surveyors and soldiers. The ships that carried the personnel were laden with timber, some ready-cut stone, lime, bricks, nails, tools and tiles. The Edina site was chosen because earlier reconnaissance had shown that there was much local rock available there for building. In 1486, the King of Portugal granted

Elmina the status of a city. The Elmina fortress was modelled on the European late medieval castle with a motte surrounded by water-filled ditch and adapted to carry cannons. Though elegant, this castle had feeble curtain walls and was ill-equipped to withstand heavy artillery bombardments.

With various European nations challenging their trade monopoly, the Portuguese were hard-pressed to modify the castle's structure. Thus in the latter part of the 16th century, drawing inspiration from Italian Renaissance fortified castles then in vogue, the Portuguese transformed the castle's system of bastions and curtain walls into formidable structures that were able to withstand onslaughts for several centuries. Basically, 15th century Castle St. Jorge comprised two fortified enclosures with a network of residential quarters, offices, workshops, store rooms, open spaces for the operations of artisans and militia, underground water cisterns etc. In Ghana, later European forts tended to follow the basic Elmina model albeit with some peculiar modifications in style, lay-out and orientation.

And outside Ghana, as the Elmina establishment chronologically antedated both Vasco da Gama's opening of the sea route to India and Christopher Columbus' voyage to America, it became the model for the creation of new trading-posts in Asia, North America, the West Indies, and other parts of Sub-Saharan Africa ■

British troops leaving Cape Coast Castle in 1873, on their way to invade the hinterland.

ARCHITECTURE

NATURE, TYPES, FUNCTIONS

The basic architectural design of the fort is a large square or rectilinear pattern. However, in some cases the fort is triangular or even irregular in shape as it is dictated by the contours of the rock on which it is built. The outer component of the fort usually comprises four bastions/batteries or towers located at the corners. The bastions were linked by means of very thick reinforced "curtain walls". The inner component comprises buildings sometimes raised to two or three storeys with or without towers, and accompanied by an enclosure, courtyard or a spur.

Three classes of fortified stations are noted in the historical architectural record during the main period of fort construction in 1482-1787, and are designated as lodge, fort, and castle. The difference lies in scale, either in terms of size, content or functional capacity. The "lodge" described as "a sort of miniature fort" and an "indefensible trading post", was small-sized, built often of earthen material or wood but sometimes of local stone. It was usually designed to be a temporary structure for small-scale trade or military purpose pending the construction of a more permanent structure. A series of early lodges built at Cape Coast, Anomabu, Butri, Jumoree, Takoradi, Apollonia and Osu are attributed to a Polish-born mercenary, Heindrick Caerlof who, in the middle to late 17th century, worked in succession for the Dutch West Indian Company, the Swedish African Company financed by Dutchmen, and the Danish African company. A typical Dutch lodge at Ankobra Hill, called Eliza Carthago and built in 1702 of local stone and fine imported Dutch yellow bricks, was excavated by the author in 1999.

The "fort" took the form of a permanent, durable structure built in brick or stone. It contained several structures for use by commandant, officers, garrison and servants and it had up to 50 guns installed in it. The vast majority of historic fortifications belong to the class of "fort". However, three others - St. Jorge at Elmina, Carolusburg at Cape Coast and

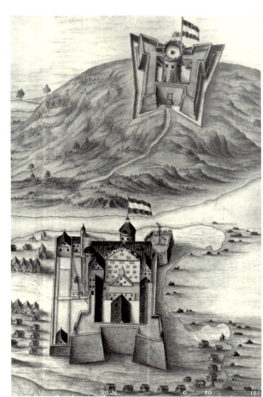

A representation of Elmina castle and Coenraadsburg fort c. 1665.

Christiansborg at Accra - are classified as "castles". Each castle covered a wider area than did a fort, was larger in size and had a more complex network of buildings. In addition, it had a capacity for a much larger population. Apart from its European staff and garrison, there could be up to 1000 slaves there at any time, as occurred in the Cape Coast and Elmina castles in the 18th century. Also, the castle was equipped with up to 100 guns and extensive logistics.

The overriding purpose of the construction of the fortifications was to secure a foothold on the coast, keep competitors as far away as possible and secure accommodation that would enable a particular nation's commercial and military staff to develop and expand their trade. Thus, nearly all the installations can be properly described as "trade forts". The exceptions are a few military forts but even these were for the protection of trade. The best examples of the military forts are the Dutch fort Coenraadsburgh, built for the defence of Elmina Castle ; Fort Kongensten at Ada and Fort Prindsensten at Keta, both built for the protection of Danish trade against local warlike people like the Awuna.

The structural arrangement in each fort from century to century was often determined by its peculiar economic specialisation (gold and/or slave trade), military specialisation, or administrative specialisation (such as serving as regional Dutch, English or Danish headquarters). For instance, whereas at Fort Coenraadsburgh the hollow bastions were used for storage of muskets and ammunition, in installations such as Fort Amsterdam at Kormantin, the bastions were used as slave dungeons or prisons ■

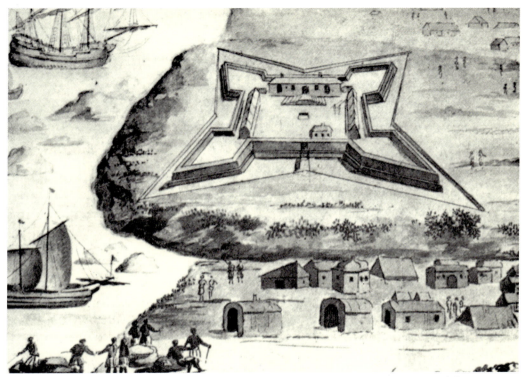

Gross Friedrichsburg fort, Brandenburg-Prussian headquarters, c. 1688.

INSIDE THE FORT

LIFE AND ORGANIZATION

Lifestyle and general organization in the fortified station has been likened to the situation on a ship. In fact the forts were sometimes described as "ships at permanent anchor".

Flags were hoisted all day as a signal to passing ships, and guns were fired in salutation whenever a ship arrived in port. A bell was rung in the daytime to announce hours of work and leisure and to regulate commerce, industry and outdoor work. At night a bell was also used to keep the soldiers on their rounds.

The daily administration in the fort was in the hands of the director-general who was assisted by a council, a chief merchant, a bookkeeper, a works superintendent, a chaplain, a physician and a school Teacher. There were also merchants, nurses, cooks, tailors, masons, carpenters and garrison members.

African slaves and servants employed at the fort lived in houses located just outside the fort and reported for duty in the daytime. Other Africans visited the fort regularly to buy and sell. African servants were employed in fort domestic services, shiploading and offloading, as canoemen, interpreters, artisans etc.

Social life in the fort could be extremely boring. This gave rise to rampant alcoholism. (The most commonly found items in archaeological excavations at forts in Ghana include schnapps, gin and wine bottles and smoking pipes!) Relations between European male staff and African women were common as there were few white women in forts. As a result, there emerged in the coastal population a sprinkling of half-breeds called "mulattoes" for whom special schools were run in the forts.

Supply of food and water often posed a problem for fort administrators, particularly in times of war or epidemics. Limited supplies of food were imported from Europe and rationed to staff. Each fort also had cisterns for storage of water collected from roofs and courtyards. Fortunately, some forts were able to contract with local merchants and 'brokers' (such as Chief Ando Wassa, of Amanfro) to provide regular supplies of yam, corn, fowl, firewood and water. Moreover, finds from archaeological research at Cape Coast Castle and Fort Coenraadsburgh have shown that castle/fort occupants were generally adequately supplied with cattle, sheep/goats, fowl, pigs and mollusca.

Sometimes forts without medical officers and staff succumbed to malaria, yellow fever, sleeping sickness etc. Hence life expectancy for Europeans in the forts was only 4 to 5 years, though some of them served for two decades or more ■

Left : The Cape Coast Castle courtyard in the 1920's.
Right : Cape Coast Castle c.1682. Europeans were confined to the castle interior, even for military drilling.

OUTSIDE THE FORT

AFRICAN-EUROPEAN RELATIONS AND IMPACT

African-European contact and interaction doubtless resulted in material enrichment at national, corporate and individual levels on both sides. In the period 1490-1560, for example nearly 1000 Kgs. of gold were exported from Mina to enrich the Portuguese crown. It is estimated that by the early 16th century, Portuguese Gold Coast trade provided 10% of the world's known gold supplies. Certainly history was made in international monetary economy when the English Royal African Company's significant gold exports in 1672 led to the minting of gold currency that bore the designation of Guinea. Even by the early 18th century, when the focus had shifted to slave trading, total European gold exports from the Gold Coast were around £ 200,000 sterling.

The infamous slave trade developed and promoted by European and Africans alike had little to commend it, morally-speaking. But it is a matter of history that slaves exported from the Gold Coast as a whole "distinguished" themselves enough to be known in the New World as "Cormantin Negroes", a name derived from the coastal port called Cormantin where the English, built their first trading-post in 1631 (later Fort Amsterdam), and turned its bastions into "the first slave-prison on the coast". It is estimated that during the 17th and 18th centuries an average of around 35,000 "Cormantinians" were exported annually from the Gold Coast. On that reckoning, roughly 7 million may have been exported during the period 1650-1850 - a colossal figure for so small a country! But the "Cormantinians" built for themselves a reputation as the most daring, stubborn and undisciplined of all the African slaves in the New World. They often spearheaded slave mutinies and the Jamaican Parliament attributed the series of mid-18th century slave revolts to "the turbulent Cormantin Negroes" notorious both for their ferocity and their dislike of farm chores and dirty work.

The international trade entailed the exchange of a great variety of imports and exports. Around 1700, the exports included slaves, gold, ivory, pepper, mahogany, salt, mats, buffalo hides and hippo tusks. A Dutch merchant observed that, in the late 17th century, some 150 different trade items were needed to adequately conduct commerce in the Gold Coast ports. The European imports included over 40 kinds of textiles, brass vessels and bracelets, iron bars, daggers, knives, swords, pikes, javelins, matchlock and fire-lock muskets, ammunition, tobacco pipes, schnapps, wine, gin, mirrors, glass beads etc. An important development that was to transform the local economy well into the colonial era was the massive importation by the Dutch of cowry shells (Cypraea moneta and annulus) from the Maldive Islands in the Indian Ocean for use as currency. Cowries had the advantage of withstanding long usage as currency and, unlike gold dust and other currencies, could not be adulterated,

Right : The bust of Queen Victoria at Cape Coast. The Queen, outraged by the beheading of general McCarthy in an ambush by the Asante, prohibited British subjects from settling on the Gold Coast.

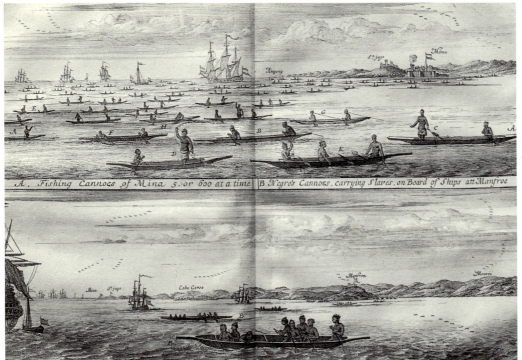

Top: fishing canoes at Elmina c. 1682.
Bottom: canoes carrying slaves on board ships at Manfroe.

defaced or counterfeited. Up until the mid-20th century, there were even some societies in Northern Ghana that insisted on cowries and cattle as bride price for the engagement of women. Given the high cost of importing goods from Europe for exchange on the Gold Coast, European companies began importing certain goods from West African locations to use in the fort exchange trade. The Dutch, in particular, promoted the coastal trade or cabotage involving trips to areas like Cape Verde, Sierra Leone, Adrar, Benin, Warri, Gabon, Loango etc., to acquire exchange items such as cotton, palm cloth, red wood, animal skins, precious stones, elephant tails etc.

The profiles of a number of local chiefs, nobility and leading merchants reflect the prosperity which came to some native communities, especially along the coast, from the international trade : Jantie Snees, employed as chief broker of the Danish fort at Cape Coast (1650-1675) on an annual salary of 150,000 dambas (£ 1,250 in modern currency !), engaged in long-distance commerce with Begho, Wenchi, Adrar, Benin etc., and supplied gold, slaves and cloth to the Danish fort and the English castle at Cape Coast as well as the Dutch castle at Elmina.

Another broker, Jan Claessen Cutta, state treasurer of Afutu State, employed by the Swedish African Company at Cape Coast (1663-1675), traded with the Danish lodge at Fredricksborg, Cape Coast Castle and Elmina Castle. Cutta was so wealthy that on one occasion the Danish commandant felt no shame in borrowing gold from him. A third man, John Kabes, Chief of Little Komenda (1690-1715), a major trader with the Royal African Company, was noted for his investments in numerous farming, fishing and salt-making enterprises and in many trading canoes. He traded on a grand scale in imported goods and slaves, gold, salt, fish and farm produce. Kabes became famous on account of the spectacular fortress mansion which he built for his use. The fort, built in European style, had bastions, 24 mounted cannons and a personal army comprising 3,000 slaves witch was at the beck and call of Kabes. A fourth business tycoon, Edward Barter of Cape Coast, was a salaried employee of the Royal African Company and had a small fort-residence with cannon and a flag flying over it and he owned a large personal army.

Dutch archives also make mention of a wealthy merchant, Badu Agyesa of Abankesieso in hinterland Denkyira, who, at the commencement of the Asante-Denkyira war of 1701, deposited 15,360 dambas of gold dust at the Shama Dutch fort for safe-keeping!

Modern Ghana's food and nutrition cultural tradition is a great beneficiary of the European fort presence and trade. A variety of food plants from different parts of the world that were cultivated by Europeans in gardens in and outside the forts subsequently spread to other part of the country - from the Mediterranean region came lemons, melons and oranges; from the New World came maize, cassava, sweet potato, groundnut, pineapple, paw-paw, guava and tannia cocoyam; from Asia came 0riental rice, water yam, taro cocoyam, plantain, banana, tamarind, coconut, and sugarcane.

Language acculturation was another outcome of the European connection. The Portuguese language continued to be used as a lingua franca in the Axim and Elmina enclaves several decades after the Portuguese had left the Gold Coast. By the late 17th century, it was reported by European authors that many canoemen in the Cape Coast and Elmina areas spoke English and Dutch well. Consequently, many European loan words and expressions were passed on to local languages ; for instance - bread (brodo), maize (eburow), calico (algodon), shoe (asopatre), sugar (esikyire), school (sukuul), church (chapul), window (frensi) etc.

The Chiefs and people of the Gold Coast, while willing to engage in trade with the Europeans were not keen on European construction of permanent forts on their

Examples of the kind of Fante flags flown by *asafo* companies - groups of warriors from the coastal areas - who formed strategic alliances with the Europeans of the forts against the Asante kingdom.
(Pix. courtesy P. Adler)

land. It had been fiercely demonstrated at the outset, when Diego d'Azambuja sought to build Elmina Castle, that the locals subscribed to a principle of equal partnership and reciprocity. When the Europeans were permitted to built permanent forts, it was on the condition that they would uphold the sovereignty of the local states. When lands were leased for fort building, documents or "notes" were prepared and given to the chiefs entitling them to retaining fees payable by the European tenants. This explains why, until colonial times, there were such designations as "Dutch Komenda", "English Komenda", "Dutch Accra", "Danish Accra", "English Accra". These arrangements were thrown into some confusion when the powerful hinterland kingdom of Asante claimed direct payment for the "notes" of forts located on territory of states which it had conquered.

The presence of so many forts on the Gold Coast naturally resulted in European domination, especially at the peak of the gold and slave trade. After the abolition of the slave trade, the organization of commerce and the maintenance of the forts became unbearably expensive. In 1850 and 1872 respectively, the Danes and Dutch sold their possessions on the coast to Britain and left. There followed a transition from the fort system to colonialism.

An interesting point in historical linguistics relates to the word Aban, a Fante Akan term meaning "walled mansion". In the early 19th century Captain George Maclean, a judicial assessor and later colonial governor, used traditional law to adjudicate cases brought to his court at Cape Coast Castle. As a result, the Cape Coast Castle Court became renown and respected for its justice. The Aban Castle became associated with the settlement of "palavers" or court cases and with the informal colonial government which emerged under Governor Maclean. The local name for castle thus became synonymous in the 19th century with Western style of government and has been used ever since to refer to the central government.

Finally, the castles and forts were the centres where the foundations were laid for Western education and Christian missionary enterprise. It was at Elmina Castle and Cape Coast Castle, from the 15th to the 17th centuries, that the first schools were established. In the 18th and 19th centuries, the process of spreading of literate culture was set in motion by Philip Quaque - chaplain and school master of Cape Coast Castle - and by the Roman Catholic missionaries of Elmina's St. Joseph's Mission. It was not without reason that Professor A.W. Lawrence wrote :

"It was along the Gold Coast that the forts had been concentrated most densely and it was not fortuitous that this was the first native African territory to become an independent state on a modern pattern ; the only generations of literate Africans that had learnt to hold their own in the whiteman's world. In all history, there is nothing comparable with the effects produced by the forts of West Africa, nowhere else have small and transitory communities of traders so changed the life of the alien peoples who surrounded them and indirectly of a vast region beyond." (Lawrence *Fortified Trade Posts 1969* : p.20-21) ∎

Right : several centuries of European presence have not succeeded in convincing the people of Cape Coast to abandon their belief in Mammy Water, an African mermaid in animist cult.

GEOGRAPHY

DISTRIBUTION AND CHRONOLOGY

Why was European commercial activity so intensely focused for nearly four centuries along Ghana's relatively small coastal area and why were so many European fortifications built there? Firstly, Ghana is unique in West Africa in being endowed with gold-rich Tarkwaian and Birrimian rock series located near the coast. Secondly, the geology of Ghana's coast between Accra and Axim is characterised by a series of rocky ridges which jut seawards as small promontories. These afford excellent building material. Moreover, the rocky coast has a number of natural harbours in the form of bays or coves as well as capes, while other areas are characterised by dangerous rocky reefs. Hence many forts were built on promontories in specific areas not far from sheltered landing places. In areas east of Accra and also west of Axim the coast is generally low, sandy and unindented, hence fort-building and control of commerce were difficult propositions. The only forts along the sandy beaches were built very late - Beyin (1756) and Keta (1784). Approximately 80 fortifications of different types were built over 300 years. Rough percentage estimates of original authorship of fortifications are as follows : Dutch 37%; English 20%; Danish 14%; Portuguese 9%; Swede 7%; French 7%; Brandenburgh-Prussia 6%.
After 1600, there was a lull in the "gold rush" momentum initiated by the Portuguese in the 15th century. New World plantation economies called for slave labour. Consequently, during the period c.1650-1810, the 'Gold Coast' became, in economic terms, more of a 'Slave Coast', requiring new, larger, more complex trade and fortification networks. This "slave economy era" which was dominated by the Dutch, English and Danes, produced the greatest number of forts which were also technically of high quality. From Axim in the west to Accra in the east, Dutch and English forts were interspersed and operated side by side in most coastal trading states and townships. From Accra eastwards to Keta, the Danes held most of the forts. It is interesting that over the entire coastal stretch of nearly 500 kilometres the distribution of forts averaged one fort per every 15 kilometres - the densest concentration of European fortifications ever recorded anywhere in the African continent ■

Above : a Spanish map of 1634 already shows twenty stations around Elmina.
Right : J.Dupuis' map from 1824.

CASTLES AND FORTS

Christiansborg Castle, Accra - Fort Good Hope, Senya Beraku
Fort Patience, Apam - Fort Amsterdam (Cormantin), Abandze
Fort William, Anomabu - Cape Coast Castle, Cape Coast
Castle St. Jorge, Elmina - Fort St. Jago, Elmina
Fort St. Sebastian, Shama - Fort Orange, Sekondi - Fort Batenstein, Butre
Fort Metal Cross, Dixcove - Gross-Friedrichsburg, Princestown
Fort St. Anthony, Axim - Fort Apollonia, Beyin

CHRISTIANSBORG CASTLE - ACCRA

1661 DENMARK   1679 PORTUGAL   1850 BRITAIN

Christiansborg Castle is unique among the castles and forts as it served as Government House during various periods in the 19th and 20th centuries and continuous to play that role today.

The building of the first lodge in the 17th century at Ursu or Osu is attributed to the Swedish African Company. In 1657, the Swedish headquarters at Carolusburg Castle, Cape Coast was captured by the Danish Guinea Company led by Heindrick Caerlof who himself was formerly the Swedish Africa Company's Commanding Director. This resulted in all Swedish establishments including Osu lodge passing into the hands of the Danish Africa Company. Caerlof defected to the Dutch in 1659. The Danish Commander of Carolusburg was tricked into believing that Denmark had been conquered. He therefore sold Carolusburg to the Dutch and with it the former Swedish establishments including Osu lodge. The Ga Paramount Chief Okaikoi, disgusted with their trickery, asked the Dutch to leave Osu. In 1661, Jost Cramer, Danish governor of Fredericksborg, near Cape Coast, acquired land from Chief Okaikoi for 3,200 gold florins. The Danes built a stone fort to replace the earthen lodge and named it Christiansborg (Christian's fortress) after the former King of Denmark, Christian IV who had died in 1648.

In 1679, Peder Bolt, a Greek who was deputy commandant at Christiansborg, instigated the murder of the Danish commandant Johan Ulrich and sold the castle to Julian de Campo Baretto, former governor of the Portuguese Island of Sao Thome. The Portuguese renamed the castle "St. Francis Xavier", garrisoned it, constructed a Roman Catholic Chapel in it and made architectural improvements on the bastions. However, the Portuguese were unpopular in Ga-land and unable to

Above : the fort c.1847.
Right : Today Christianborg Castle is the seat of the Presidency of Ghana, refered to as "The Castle". Both views show the east and north sides.

withstand English and Dutch trade competition. They thus resold the castle to the Danes in 1683. Two years later, when Fort Fredericksborg was sold to the English, Christiansborg became the Danish headquarters.

At this time, the warlike Akwamu were in control of the Accra region. In 1693, a notable Akwamu trader, Asameni, formerly a cook in Danish service, led some Akwamu customers to the castle ostensibly to trade. The castle factor and staff were tricked and overpowered. The commandant, Nicolaus Janssen, severely wounded, took refuge at the Dutch Fort Crevecœur. Asameni acquired booty worth 1,400 marks in gold. He assumed the governorship of the castle and donned the Danish governor's uniform. Above the castle, he flew a blue flag with the image of an African warrior brandishing a dagger. Asameni invited captains of privately-owned English and Dutch ships to trade with him and he entertained them lavishly, his castle guns booming salute to them. In June 1694, however, two Danish ships arrived to redeem the castle for 50 marks. Asameni left the castle, taking with him the keys which henceforth became part of the Akwamu stool property.

The 18th Century witnessed a new burst of Danish fort-building. From Teshi eastward as far as Keta, they built a chain of subordinate forts and lodges which enhanced the importance of Christiansborg. At this time, trade in gold from Akyem and elsewhere was on the increase at the castle. Much gold was exported by the Danes and minted in ducats in Denmark. The ducats bore the icon of the castle and the superscription "Christiansborg". Nevertheless, the trade in slaves was predominant. Hundreds of slaves were auctioned at a slave market at Osu, (the auctioneer's platform is still visible in extant old houses), and driven through a dark tunnel to the castle's dungeons to await shipment.

In 1788, the Danes at Christiansborg, disgusted with the slave trade, initiated development of plantations in the Akuapem escarpment area for cultivation of coffee,

Left : north side of the Castle.
Above left : double arcade entrance leading to the Castle.
Above right : main entrance leading to the courtyard of the Castle.
Next pages : the main yard in 1847 and today.

cotton, etc., as export crops in place of slaves. The scheme proved to be unsuccessful. With Denmark's abolition of the slave trade in 1803, general trade decline set in at Christiansborg. In 1850, all Danish possessions on the Gold Coast were sold to Britain and the Danes left. Architecturally, the early 18th century Christiansborg Castle was partly anachronistic featuring a pointed diminutive southeast bastion and an equally archaic northeast bastion. It became necessary to rebuild these. In addition, new powerful bastions were built in the southwest and northwest areas; new store rooms and garrison quarters were constructed and internal buildings were renovated.

A Danish officer, Romer, gives an eye-witness account of the castle as seen in 1760: "It is a massive and uncommonly strong building; all the warehouses are vaulted and the walls are four cubits (nearly 3 metres) thick. It used to be an absolutely regular fort with four bastions and made a square of 60 cubits. The battlements were 18 - 20 cubits high and 12 cubits wide and occupied with some 40 iron cannons. We could not find place for many goods, especially when we received by each ship 30 - 40,000 pots of brandy.

We set the vessels with brandy in the rooms of the servants who imposed a heavy leakage, or rather 'drinkage'."

The castle inherited by the British in 1850 has been described by one architectural historian as structurally very irregular, "an incongruous huddle of buildings one on top of another, or one outside of the other".

After 1876, British colonial governors took residence in the castle and then abandoned it between 1890-1901, during which time it functioned first as a constabulary mess and then as a lunatic asylum. Happily, in 1902, it reverted to its status as seat of government. It was at this time that a comprehensive rehabilitation was undertaken - new upper storeys were installed in consonance with the 17th century Danish substructure ■

FORT GOOD HOPE - SENYA BERAKU

1705 NETHERLANDS   1868 BRITAIN

Thanks to their establishment of a lodge at Senya Beraku in 1667, the Dutch entered into a long-standing relationship with the Agona State. Its chief subsequently requested the Dutch to build a permanent fort at Beraku. The Dutch accepted the invitation because of the prospect of a trade boom in gold, ivory and slaves emanating from the Akyem kingdom located in the hinterland beyond Agona, and also because private traders were taking advantage of the absence of any Dutch forts in the area between Accra and Apam.

In 1705-06, as a preliminary stage prior to building a four-sided fort, the Dutch constructed a small triangular fort on a promontory located near a cove where there was a good landing beach. As the fort appealed to presage great expectations, the Dutch named it 'De Goede Hoop', meaning "Good Hope".

The triangular fort had three bastions located at the southwest, southeast and

Top left : The fort c.1820 flying the Dutch flag.
Below left : aerial view today
Above : view from the southeast bastion.
Right : the town of Senya Beraku below the fort.

Meanwhile, the expected gold trade boom from Akyem did not materialise. However, the trade in slaves expanded considerably due partly to the increase in prisoners from inter-ethnic wars in the area involving Asante, Akyem, Akwamu etc. By 1715, the fort's limited size could not cope with the volume of slave trade.

It therefore became necessary to double the size of the fort and give it a square or rectangular outline. Along the north and west, curtains were built and a bastion created at their junction.

Next, the diagonal wall built of earthen material was removed. Later on, a large male slave prison was created in the southwest bastion. Around a large central courtyard were ranged apartments and hall for officers and garrison, stores, kitchens, granary, a female prison and a powder magazine. In the second half of the 18th century, an outer wall was built round the fort.

In a fitting tribute, an official report of 1804 described Fort Goede Hoop as "one of the finest and most spacious forts on the coast". The Dutch abandoned the fort, in 1816, and during the 1868 exchange of forts, it reverted to Britain ■

northeast corners, with a long diagonal curtain wall between the southeast and northeast bastions. An apartment building was erected behind the south curtain.

Left page : view from a southern-facing embrasure.
Above left : view of courtyard from the female slave prison.
Above : "A good landing beach…".

FORT PATIENCE - APAM

1697 NETHERLANDS   1868 BRITAIN

In the late 17th century, the small state of Acron - sandwiched between the larger British allies of Agona and Fante - sought to have a strong fort built on its territory to defend it in case of attack. The Dutch, while willing to erect a fort at Apam, were in no position to build a large one. Building of the fort commenced in 1697 on the summit of a promontory close to a sheltered beach and bay. However, disagreement between the two sides concerning the form of the fort delayed its completion until 1702. Hence the name they gave to the fort - Lijdzaamheid, meaning patience.
The initial structure was a "small two-storey house". Between 1701 and 1721, this was strengthened with two demi-bastions at diametrically opposite corners.

Top left : the fort c.1704.
Above : The fort is now a rest house.
Right : Aerial view from northeast.

The northwest bastion was solid while the southeast bastion was hollow and used as a male slave prison. (There was also a small female prison underneath the two-storey building).

A small courtyard and spur in front of the two-storey building had ranged round it apartments for various fort officers, store rooms, a guard room etc. Two large service yards were built as adjuncts to the main fort complex and included kitchens and the "Orange Hall" for receptions or "palavers". Initially, the economy of Fort Patience showed good promise. It was reported in November 1705, that two Dutch ships, the Peynenburgh and the Christina, had loaded a total of nearly 900 slaves at Apam, Beraku and Accra within two months.

However, subsequently, trade became limited to slave commerce due to war between Akyem and Akwamu. Later, there ensued war between the Asante allies of the Dutch and Akyem, who were hostile to the Dutch. As a result in 1811, the Akyem attacked and destroyed Fort Patience, and threw its guns over the walls.

In 1868, the Dutch transferred the fort to Britain. The fort has been kept in good

condition in the twentieth century largely because it has been used as a police station and a post office and more recently as a rest house ∎

Above left : A beautiful bay lies to the east of the fort.
Below left : main gate leading to the courtyard.
Above : staircase in the courtyard leading to the Orange Hall.
Right : the fort at sunset.

FORT AMSTERDAM (CORMANTIN) - ABANDZE

1638 BRITAIN   1665 NETHERLANDS

History has it that, in 1631, a renegade employee of the Dutch West Indian Company called Arent Groote, acting on behalf of the English Company of Adventurers Trading to Guynney and Binney, signed an agreement with the Chief of Cormantin by which a hill site near the village was ceded to the English company. That year, a lodge was built by the company. Later, it was destroyed by fire and the company converted the lodge into a fort in 1638. In 1661, ownership of the fort was transferred to the Royal African Company and it became the headquarters of the English possessions on the Gold Coast.

In 1665, the Dutch Admiral De Ruyter captured Fort Cormantin in retaliation for the capture of several Dutch forts by English Admiral Holmes in 1664. The Dutch reconstructed the fort and renamed it "Fort Amsterdam". The English transferred their headquarters to Cape Coast Castle.

In 1811, the Anomabu people, allies of the English, attacked and destroyed the fort. It was never reoccupied and was left in ruins until the Ghana Museums and Monuments Board restored it in 1951. Structurally, the Cormantin fort may be characterised as follows :

It was rectangular in outline with two square bastions and two round bastions at the corners linked by curtain walls. Around a central courtyard were arranged (a) a one-storeyed building on the western side, (b) a two-storeyed building along the northern side and (c) a line of two or three-storeyed buildings on the southern side.

While the curtain and bastion on the northern side were solidly built, the others were constructed with an earth filling between two walls of stone laid in mortar. This unsatisfactory building procedure later resulted in cracks and disintegration at the time of abandonment of the fort. The southeast bastion, deliberately designed to be hollow, had a grated ventilation in the roof and was used as a slave prison - believed to be the first of its kind on the Gold Coast.

It is said that slaves taken from this prison for export to the Caribbean Islands

Top : the fort c.1704
Below : the fort today
Right : children standing on the site of the ancient enclosure wall.

were dubbed "Coromantese" or "Cormantins".

Trade at Fort Amsterdam experienced considerable up-and-down trends. During the period 1705-1716, for instance, trade figures were given as 481 marks of gold and 149 slaves and it was said that "At Cormantin there has always been good

trade". At other times however, there were complaints that "there is little trade" because of wars and because the local chief and people had leased the site to Britain and not Holland. Hence the Dutch had no jurisdiction there and, whenever it suited them, the Cormantin people blocked the trade routes until the Dutch had paid large sums of money.

In 1704, William Bosman expressed great reservations about Fort Amsterdam's future : "A moderate charge would improve this fortress; but the commerce of the place not being sufficient to bear the expense, it is better to let it alone"■

Left : looking eastward
Above : looking south through the great hall openings.
Left page : the fort on its promontory

FORT WILLIAM - ANOMABU

1753-70 BRITAIN

Anomabu became the focus of intense European trade rivalry in the 17th and 18th centuries, partly because of its easy access to a rich hinterland and partly because the local Anomabu were themselves powerful and astute traders. From the middle of the 17th century, European companies vied with each other in the quest for rights to establish and maintain a trading post at Anomabu. The earliest lodge was built in 1640 by the Dutch using earthwork, changed hands four times - from the Dutch to Swedes, then to the Danes, back to the Dutch and finally to the English.

In 1674, the English built a small fort using more durable materials and called it Charles, after the reigning monarch King Charles II. However, it was abandoned in order to concentrate efforts and costs on Fort Carolusburg at Cape Coast. Even though the English demolished Fort Charles in 1731 to prevent its capture and use by another European company, the French sneaked in and built a fort where Fort Charles once stood.

In 1698, the English Royal African Company "licensed" ship captains not in its employment upon the payment of a 10% "affiliation fee" to enable them to trade in its areas of monopoly. There followed a flood of "Ten Percenters" trading at English forts, often outnumbering the company's own ships. Anomabu became a popular haunt of "ten percenters", (until their licensing was stopped in 1712), exporting vast numbers of slaves.

The Dutch director-general at Elmina, Engelgraaf Robbertsz, quoting an English captain on Anomabu Slave trade exports stated in 1717 : "From January 1702 to

Above : the fort c.1682
Left : the northeast bastion was specifically built to hold slaves.
Right : the beach where the Asante armies reached the ocean for the first time in 1802.

August 1708 they took to Barbados, Jamaica a total of not less than 30,141 slaves and in this figure are not included transactions made for other ships sailing to such Islands as Nevis, Montserrat, St. Christopher, for the South Sea Company, the New Netherlands and others which would increase the above number considerably, and of which Annemaboe alone could provide about one third."

Between 1753 and 1770, the English built an entirely new fort close to the former location of Fort Charles. They used local as well as imported bricks and lime. The new fort was not named until the 19th century when a storey was added to it during the reign of King William IV and it was called Fort William.

It was built on an eroded shelf of hard rock close to a sandy beach indentation with a sheltered anchorage. Structurally, Fort William was almost a square, having larger bastions in the northeast and southeast and smaller bastions in the southwest and northwest corners. The bastions and curtain walls were solidly built of bricks. The inner apartments, including the three-storied main building complex, were constructed of stone, and bricks were used for vaulting and coigning.

Concerning its design and plan, it has been said that "nowhere else does the original structure of a fort include a large prison specifically built to hold slaves awaiting transport overseas". The northeast bastion, designed as a slave prison,

Left page : aerial view today.
Above left : inmates returning to the prison after their chores.
Left : looking eastward.
Above right : the main courtyard.

had a string of tall vaults, a rock floor, high, dark walls and a constantly cool temperature. As an architectural model, Fort William has been acclaimed as one of the most elegant and best built forts of the coast. Compared to other late 18th and 19th century Gold Coast forts, it also had the best stock of cannons, qualitatively and quantitatively.

It is not without reason that it has served Anomabu and Ghana well in recent times as a rest house, post office, and prison ■

CAPE COAST CASTLE - CAPE COAST

1653 SWEDEN   1665 BRITAIN

Above : the fort in 1873.
Centre and right : the waves breaking against the rocks east and west made the fort easy to defend.

The strategic location of Cape Coast having a sheltered beach in proximity to Elmina Castle made it a great attraction to the European nations. Hence, for nearly a century, there was a ding-dong competition among the Portuguese, Dutch, Danes, Swedes and English to gain control of Cape Coast. The Portuguese built the first trade lodge in 1555 and called the local settlement "Cabo Corso", meaning short cape, later corrupted to Cape Coast. The Swedes, led by Krusenstjerna, built a permanent fort in 1653 and called it Carolusburg after King Charles X of Sweden. During the next 11 years, the Danes, the local Fetu chief and the Dutch each in turn captured nd held Carolusburg for a time. Finally, the English fleet led by Captain Holmes took Carolusburg. The fort remained in English hands till the late 19th century serving as the West African headquarters seat of the president of the Committee of Merchants and later as the seat of the British governor.

Jean Barbot, in an eye-witness account of the form of the late 17th century Carolusburg after it had been transformed by

the English Chartered Company of Royal Adventurers from a fort into a castle, wrote : "The lodgings and apartments within the castle are very large and well-built of brick, having three fronts which with the platform on the south almost make a quadrangle answering to the inside of the walls and form a very handsome place of arms, well-paved; under which is a spacious mansion or place to keep the slaves in, cut out of the rocky ground, arched and divided into several rooms so that it will conveniently contain a thousand blacks let down at an opening made for the purpose. The keeping of the slaves underground is a good security to the garrison against any insurrection."

In 1996, Professor Anquandah's archaeological excavations at Cape Coast Castle unearthed structural remains of the 17th and 18th century Swedish and English brick fortress under the modern castle's courtyard pavement. The findings retrieved included hundreds of red bricks, roof tiles, imported European pottery, glass beads, liquor, perfume and ointment bottles, gun parts, local pottery, indigenous milling stones, bones of cattle, sheep, fish, birds, molluscs and graves of English officers.

Left : the courtyard where P. Quaque is buried. Later, Gov. McLean and his wife were also buried there.
Above : The Smith's Tower cannons kept the African town in check.

In the period 1766-73, the British Committee of Merchants which was responsible for the administration of British forts, undertook a major rehabilitation of the castle and gave it its present-day form. The 18th century castle was built of local quarried sandstone rock. Doors, window openings and vaults were given brick dressings. In plan, the castle has an irregular polygon shape. Its major features include a large pentagonal courtyard overlooking the sea, with one long side and two short sides enclosed by low curtain walls on the seaward side and the two landward sides enclosed by three-storey ranges of buildings. Each of the five corners of the pentagon has polygonal bastions. The castle's habitable accommodation area covers 3,900 metres square. In 1672, the English King Charles II granted a new charter to the Royal African Company for developing Guinea trade. A period of expansion of trade in gold and slaves ensued and this was reflected in the large-scale production and circulation of the famous British gold currency called the Guinea which bore the emblem of the Royal African Company. It is estimated that around 1700, the Company was exporting some 70,000 slaves per annum, to the New World. When the slave trade was abolished, the castle became an important conduit for development of legitimate

trade. In the period 1830-50, the following figures of the Castle's average annual exports were recorded :

18,000 ounces of gold, 40-50 tons of ivory, 80,000 pounds of pepper, 130,000 pounds of coffee, 35,000 bushels of corn and some 70 tons of camwood. Imports were listed as including metal ware, cotton goods, rum, tobacco, guns and ammunition.

Cape Coast Castle shares honours with Elmina Castle and Christiansborg Castle as a pioneering centre for western education in modern Ghana. In the early 1750's, an Anglican Minister, Thomas Thompson, established the first primary school at Cape Coast Castle. Thompson arranged for a Cape Coast youth, Philip Quaque to receive ministerial training in

England by the British Society for the Propagation of the Gospel. Quaque became chaplain and school master at Cape Coast Castle. In 1787, a local education authority called the Torridzonian Society (T.Z.S) was founded at Cape Coast Castle under the Presidency of the Governor for promoting local education. T.Z.S raised funds to expand the Cape Coast Castle school system. For the first time in Gold Coast history, children were provided with school uniforms. Cape Coast Castle was brightened with children wearing blue jackets with red cuffs and capes to which were affixed badges marked T.Z.S and they also wore trousers, shorts, black cravats and hats. It was as if the 18th century English urban school had been transplanted to Cape Coast!

In the 1870's, Cape Coast Castle became the headquarters of the West Indian Regiment, (mainly Jamaican, recruited by the British to help fight the Asante). The syncopated black brass band music the West Indian regimental bands played in their spare time sparked a response by the local British-trained Cape Coast brass band musicians to "do their own thing". In the 1880's, local Fante musicians therefore created "Adaha" music - the earliest documented example of Ghanaian highlife music style.

In recent times Cape Coast Castle has served as a school, a historical museum and the regional headquarters of the Ghana Museums and Monuments Board ■

Left and centre : commemorating the tragic fate of our ancestors.
Right : a strong defence.

ELMINA CASTLE - ELMINA

1482 PORTUGAL 1637 NETHERLANDS 1872 BRITAIN

The Portuguese founded Castle "Sao Jorge da Mina" in 1482 to protect the gold-rich lands discovered in 1471. The castle was completed according to its original plan in 1486 and the town was raised to the status of a "city".

The castle's site was carefully selected by Portuguese navigators, because it was strategically located at the end of a narrow promontory bounded on two sides by the Atlantic Ocean and the Benya River or lagoon. Here, in the lee of a low headland, a natural harbour provided sheltered anchorage.

During the 15th and 16th centuries, the Portuguese enjoyed a trade boom in spite of numerous attempts by Castilians and later the French and the English to break the Portuguese trade monopoly.

Left : Elmina castle and Coenraadsburg fort c. 1840
Above : Elmina castle and Coenraadsburg fort today.
Right : the fishing harbour behind Elmina castle.

Above and left : The bay offered one of the best anchorages in West Africa.
right : The brick sundial built by the Dutch in 1679.
Next pages : Panoramic view from the tower.

The Portuguese imported vast quantities of old and new cloths, blankets and linen from Morocco, North European copper and brassware, millions of "manillas" (metal bracelets) and iron kettles and bars in exchange for gold dust and ornaments supplied by Mina. So extensive and popular was the cloth trade that a factor maintained a large shop for old linen c.1500-1507. The commander of the castle wrote to King Manuel in 1503 : "Sir, I, Diego d'Alvarenga, kiss the royal hands of your highness and I report that I have received the old linen."
The import trade raised the issue of porterage as the natives needed assistance in conveyance of large quantities of European goods into the hinterland and coastlands. To meet this need, the Portuguese initiated, in the early 16th century, the importation of slaves from Benin to Elmina in exchange for gold, ivory etc.
As it turned out, however, the price of gold slumped in Europe in the 16th century due to massive importation of superior gold from Mexico. At the same time, the Portuguese Crown spent vast sums of resources on defensive works, artillery, galleys, warships and convoys related to Mina. Thus weakened, the Portuguese succumbed to Dutch attacks and were dislodged from Elmina in 1637.

Left. the male slave prison of Elmina.
Above : the door of no return.

Until that date, Elmina Castle had served as the headquarters of the Portuguese West African possessions. Hence forward and until 1872, it became the headquarters of the Dutch possessions in the Gold Coast. It was during the Dutch era that Elmina reached the high-water mark of its evolution. The native "city" which sprang up directly to the west of the castle expanded and the population is estimated to have risen from 4,000 in the early 17th century to 10,000 in the late 17th century and 15,000 in the 18th century, partly due to the impact of the gold and especially the slave trade. From the standpoint of architectural history, the Elmina Castle was renown as the first major European building constructed in tropical Africa. During the period 1550-1637, the Portuguese rebuilt the castle's northern and western corners, the great courtyard and the north bastion. In the Dutch period, the Portuguese Church was turned into an auction hall, a new Dutch chapel was built and much rebuilding took place, especially in the north and west bastions and the riverside yard.

Jean Barbot who authored the book - *a Description of the Coasts of North and South Guinea* (1732), visited Elmina Castle and participated in Easter worship at the Dutch chapel. He gave an eye-witness account in 1682 :

"This castle has justly become famous for beauty and strength, having no equal on all the coasts of Guinea. Built square with very high walls of dark brown stone so very firm that it may be said to be cannon-proof. On the land side it has two canals always furnished with rain or fresh water sufficient for the use of the garrison and the ships-canals cut in the rock by the Portuguese (by blowing up the rock little by little with gunpowder).

Left : the castle cell for those condemned to death.
Center : the main courtyard.
Above : the Portuguese chapel, later transformed by the Dutch into an auction hall, viewed from the Governor's Hall.
Right page : the north bastion view of Coenraadsburg fort.

The warehouses either for goods or provisions are very largely and stately always well furnished." Around 1774, when the Dutch completed the castle reconstruction and consolidation, the total habitable accommodation within its wall was 3,950 m2, including new buildings in the large riverside yard (500 metres square) which, according to Dutch Company soldier Michael Hemmersam, were specially put up for rearing of civet cats whose odorous secretions were twice weekly extracted for the perfume industry so vital "in those times of little washing."

In 1872, Elmina Castle was ceded by the Dutch to Britain. Since then it has served a variety of purposes : For many years it housed the Ghana Police Recruit Training Centre. In 1972, it was taken over by the Ghana Museums and Monuments Board and was included by UNESCO on the World Heritage List. Recently, it has been used by the Edinaman Secondary School and now has a historical museum exhibition themed "Images of Elmina Across the Centuries".

The historic name of Elmina has become immortalised in New World history and culture, manifesting itself in the "Mina Nations" of the Caribbean and South American black Diaspora. The "Mina Nations" were ethnic clubs that invoked ancestral spirits and preserved the language, arts, culture and cults of the West African slaves shipped to the New World from Elmina ■

FORT ST. JAGO (COENRAADSBURG) - ELMINA

1660'S NETHERLANDS   1872 BRITAIN

In 1503, according to historical narration by the Portuguese Diego de Alvarenga, a Portuguese missionary converted and baptized the paramount chief of the Efutu Kingdom on the Mina coast together with 300 of his subjects. The chief permitted the Portuguese to build a church on the hill located opposite the Castle St. Jorge. The site was dedicated to the Portuguese saint, Jago.

In 1637, the Dutch employed the hill as a gun-position to bombard and take Elmina Castle from the Portuguese. The following year, the Dutch, seeking to protect the castle from the landward side, built on St. Jago hill, 33 metres above sea level, a redoubt or fortified quadrilateral earthwork with a tower and gate and a single-storeyed building within a courtyard all surrounded by an embankment. In the 1660's, the Dutch used local sandstone rock to build a permanent fort to replace the earthen fortification which was then destroyed.

The stone fort, named Coenraadsburg, is unique and impressive as "the oldest

purely military architecture of the Gold Coast". It had no commercial warehouses of any kind and its military fortifications were based on the design of baroque military architecture. Its salient features comprised two giant, strong landward bastions on the northeast and northwest sides for defending the castle from land attacks and two smaller seaward bastions on the southwest and southeast sides. The bastions were linked by curtain walling. Two-storeyed apartments on the landward side and a single storey on the seaward side

Right : the fort c. 1682
Above : view of Elmina from Coenraadsburg fort.
Right page : today the fort is a rest house.

were built around a courtyard. These apartments accommodated a garrison of 69 officers and soldiers who came on rotation duty from the castle. Other rooms served as kitchen, gun magazine and prisons for disciplining European convicts of the Dutch Company.

The entire fortification and residential complex was surrounded by an outer wall equipped with many arched gun ports. (A number of 19th century cannon can still be seen at the fort today).

Sentry boxes are located at the tops of the bastions and a high watch tower located at the gateway was used for hoisting flags for signaling to ships approaching Elmina. A ravelin, or half-moon, outwork located in front of the fort is linked to the main entrance by a drawbridge overhanging a shallow ditch. Near the entrance are two inscriptions in Dutch recording, firstly the name of the fort as Coenraadsburg and its 'Builder' as the Elmina Castle Director General J. Valckenburgh (1667) and, secondly, that of Director General Dirck Wilsree who commissioned the fort's outer walls in 1671.

Historical archives indicate that from the 1640's, the general area of St. Jago's hill slopes served as cattle pastures, a vegetable salad and fruit garden and a place of relaxation for Elmina Castle's European staff.

In 1880, eight years after the Dutch transfer of the fort to the British, several modifications and extensions were carried out by the British which facilitated the use of the fort for civilian pursuits. For instance, a third floor was added to the 17th century two-storeyed landward apartments and rooms were added to the seaward apartment complex. The fort was used in the 19th and 20th centuries as a prison, hospital and rest house.

Archaeological research conducted at the site in the 1990s has revealed remains of the 16th century Portuguese Church, many 17th to 19th century European imported goods and African milling equipment, pottery and food remains ■

FORT ST. SEBASTIAN - SHAMA

1520'S PORTUGUESE   1638 NETHERLANDS   1872 BRITAIN

Above : the fort c.1786
Right : aerial view
Right page : the fort as it would have been seen from the mast of a trading ship centuries ago.

Fort St. Sebastian was originally constructed and named by the Portuguese c.1520-26. However, its first appearance on a map was in the context of Di Castaldi's Venetian map of 1564. In putting up the fort, the Portuguese hoped to stop English ships from interfering in their trade in the Shama area.

According to a Portuguese chart of 1630, the Portuguese fort had a bastion, two single-storeyed buildings with pitched roofs and a two-storeyed tower. At the time the Dutch took over the fort it was in a state of ruin. While retaining its name, they carried out repairs in 1640-42 and added substantially to the previous structural form.

The salient structural features of the Dutch phase were : an inner rectangular enclosure, pointed bastions located at opposite northwest and southeast corners, smaller round towers located at opposite southwest and northeast corners, an inner

courtyard around which were lined two storeys of rooms on the northeast and northwest sides, a single storey of vaulted rooms with battery on the southwest side and a spur.

Fort St. Sebastian is of major historical interest in the sphere of early architectural studies because its residuary Portuguese work seems to rival that of Elmina Castle itself, while its later Dutch work is remarkably complete even to the extent of the preservation of a 17th century turret at the apex of a bastion. Indeed, however much the Dutch may have modified them, the southwest round tower with gunports, the northeast round tower and the curtain walls which link these towers and enclose the inner courtyard are clearly survivals from the Portuguese period. The early Shama architectural design appears to be a small-scale copy of Elmina Castle, a square courtyard with round towers at two opposite angles. Similarly, the fortifications were given greater solidity and power on the landward than the seaward side because of the notorious turbulence of the local people.

From Dutch West Indian records, it is evident that the fort received some gold and slaves from Adom, Wassa, Twifo and other local agencies for export. However, on the whole its commercial output was minimal. A dispatch from Elmina to Dutch overseas headquarters dated 13th November 1705 stated : "Chama is good for water and fuel wood but there is no trade".

Indeed the Shama environment, like that of Butre, was ideal for collecting and milling wood for supply to ships and forts and the Dutch made this a cornerstone of their policy. Also from the early 18th century, the Dutch initiated sugar and cotton plantation and milling schemes in the fertile river valleys of Shama so as to make the area more economically viable.

In 1872, the fort was ceded to Britain. Unfortunately, not much attention was

Above : the male slave prison is now used by the Community Tribunal.
Above left and left page : the main courtyard
Next two pages : Fort Saint Sebastian today.

paid to it and decay set in. It was not till 1957 that it was rehabilitated and almost restored to its Dutch period status ■

FORT ORANGE - SEKONDI

1670'S NETHERLANDS   1872 BRITAIN

The coast at Sekondi became another theatre of European trade competition in the 17th and 18th centuries. The competition often degenerated into hostilities as local Ahanta peoples were ranged in opposing alliances supporting the English or Dutch companies in their two separate trade posts located within gun shot of each other. For instance, in 1694, one Ahanta group captured and destroyed the Dutch fort which then had to be rebuilt; in 1698 a second group of Ahanta captured and damaged the English fort and the English had to rebuild it only for it to be recaptured by the French in 1779.

The foundation of the earliest-known Dutch lodge harks back to the 1670's. The precise date is uncertain. However, by 1704, the lodge had become a small fort called "Oranje".
Initially, the fort had two bastions; one

Above left : the fort c.1709
Above : a view of the fort from the north.
Right : the fort has been used as a lighthouse since 1872.

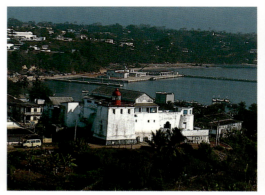

located in the north and the other in the southwest. In the course of the 18th century, there were improvements so that, at its later stages, the fort's architectural features included the following : a square enclosure, within it and arranged around a central courtyard, a group of two-storeyed buildings and a group of one-storeyed buildings ; functionally these included apartments for the commandant and other officers, a warehouse, kitchen, gunpowder magazine, slave prison, service yard etc ; fortifications including bastions at the four corners with cannons and gunports directed towards the nearby English fort.

The economic history of the fort was insubstantial : a 1711 audit report from Elmina Castle headquarters indicated that between 1705 and 1716, main trade export figures amounted to 300 marks of gold and 151 slaves. Although this record was a little better than the outputs of Moure, Cormantin, Butre and Commany, Fort Orange was nevertheless classified as among the non-viable Dutch forts and it had to be abandoned in 1840 for a time. To supplement its economic output, the Dutch established in 1703 a cotton plantation and industry nearby. On the whole, the trade performance of the fort was assessed as mediocre to poor and this was attributed above all to blockage of the trade routes by the Wassa and other local groups and continual harassment by hostile Ahanta.

Fort Orange was ceded to Britain in 1872 and was subsequently used as a lighthouse ∎

Above left : aerial view from the north.
Above right : aerial view from the south.
Centre : the main entrance.
Right : Sekondi fishing harbour below the fort.

FORT BATENSTEIN - BUTRE

1656 NETHERLANDS   1872 BRITAIN

Butre village is located in a sheltered bay amidst the forests of Ahantaland, east of Cape Three Points. Like Dixcove and Friedricksburg, it was among the early historic settlements generated by the 17th century inter-European and inter-African conflicts, partly because it lay close to the gold-rich hinterland. As early as 1598, the Dutch West Indian Company established a trade post at Butre. As a counterpoise, the Dutch-financed Swedish Africa Company led by Heinrich Caerlof set up a lodge at Butre in 1650-52. In retaliation, the W.I.C. instigated the Ankasa people to attack and expel the Swedish Company.

Then, in 1656, the Dutch Company constructed its own fort on the hill at Butre and named it Batenstein. The fort was visited and described by 17th century authors, Jean Barbot in 1679 and William Bosman in 1701. Bosman said of it : "On a very high hill lies a tiny ill-designed fort called Batenstein with four useless little bastions upon which are mounted eleven light cannon." It had a pair of flat-roofed

buildings adjoining the bastions. So feeble was the structure, militarily, that it was said that it was shaken itself whenever it had to fire its own guns. In reality, its guns were used more for firing salutes than actual military encounters because the fort's commanding location on top of the steep hill gave it a semblance of impregnability that tended to put off would-be invaders.

In the late 18th century, it was rebuilt and given new structural additions. For instance, the bastions were reshaped; the eastern bastions were amalgamated into

Centre : The fort c.1709.
Above : view of the village from the main entrance.
Right : Today the fort is in ruins.

one strong battery; the northwestern bastion was expanded; and the amorphous apartments rehabilitated into a two-storied building.

The prospects of flourishing trade envisaged by the Dutch Company never really materialised. Hague archives contain several letters dispatched from Elmina Castle to West Indian Company headquarters in which there were dismal complaints: "At Boutry there is little trade because those of Wassa block the passages". This was largely due to political instability engendered by local wars. For instance, Boerhave, Dutch commandant at Butre wrote in August 1711 "John Connie, headman of the Brandenburg natives is more and more chasing away our subject peoples, robbing some of them, killing others."

For the entire period of 11 years (1705-16), Butre's main trade export figures were limited to 156 slaves and 290 marks of gold. No wonder the Butre fort was abandoned during the period 1818-1829.

Even though Butre was unsuccessful as a trading station, it was almost indispensable as a "service-fort". Located in an almost round-the-year rainfall zone with a luxuriant tropical rain forest, it was prolific in timber production and saw-milling. Logs were conveyed along the nearby River Batenstein to be used in construction and repair work for Dutch forts and ships. Besides, Butre Bay became a busy "harbour" for small Dutch ships needing refitting and rehabilitation.

Furthermore, the Dutch Company, long before the abolition of the slave trade and enforcement of legitimate trade, had embarked on sugar plantation/mill projects and coffee and cotton plantation schemes in the Butre district.

In 1872, Fort Batenstein was handed over to Britain which had it demilitarized and it virtually fell into ruins ■

Above left: though it was set on an almost impregnable position, the fort was never used for military purposes.
Above: the main gateway.
Right: ocean view from the fort.

FORT METAL CROSS - DIXCOVE

1692 BRITAIN   1868 NETHERLANDS   1872 BRITAIN

In the 1680's, the Ahantaland around Infuma settlement was a bone of contention between the English and the Brandenburgers. The English were determined to acquire land there to build a fort because many English interloper captains were accustomed to trading at Fort Gross Friedrichsburg to the detriment of English commerce.

The chief of Upper/Greater Dixcove leased to the English a promontory site near Infuma village, located on the shore of a large and sheltered bay, later designated as Dick's Cove (Dixcove). The Cove's calm waters and sandy beach made it an ideal "harbour" for canoes and small boats while ships could anchor about 3 kilometres offshore. The Royal African Company commenced construction of the fort in 1692 but was unable to complete it until 1698 because of spasmodic attacks by the Ahanta people which continued well into the 18th century on account of the presence of the Dutch fort Babenstein at Butre.

The original fort, as seen and described by writers like Jean Barbot, was square with a pointed bastion at each corner except for the southwest corner which had a round tower. The bastions and tower were linked by curtain walls. The inner structure comprised apartments, storage rooms and kitchen arranged round a small courtyard. Subsequently there were several alterations to the original structure : a spur ending with a bastion which was constructed in the 18th century consisted of garrison apartments, storage rooms and a workshop. One of the hollow bastions in the main section of the fort was employed as a slave prison. By 1750, the fort was equipped to carry up to 25 canons.

Concerning the economic value of the fort, it must be said that it was never commercially viable. During the 17th and 18th centuries, the gold obtained from the Dixcove hinterland for export by the fort was of inferior quality.

After the abolition of the slave trade, the fort's commerce declined. Only limited quantities of gold, ivory, and palm oil

Above : the fort c.1709
Below and right page : no other fort survived as many sieges as the English fort at Dixcove.
Next pages : left, the governor's tower overlooking the slave prisons. Right, view of the village from the northeast bastion.

were available for export in exchange for imported textiles, metal bars, rum and gunpowder. Indeed, a Parliamentary report of 1817 stated that in terms of trade profitability, Dixcove had become "a laughing stock".

Why then was Fort Dixcove not abandoned? The answer lay in the several natural assets that Infuma and its surrounding forest lands had: the area produced substantial quantities of quality lime, timber, and limestone as well as locally-made bricks - all vital resources for building operations in the various English forts. Hence, Dixcove Fort became for the English an indispensable service fort, much like the Dutch fort Batenstein at Butre. Small ships anchored there in the bay to undergo repairs.

In 1867, the Dixcove area was transferred to Dutch suzerainty and the fort was renamed Metalen Kruis (Brass Cross) after one of the gun-boats sent from Holland to put down uprisings by native peoples who refused to accept the British-Dutch exchange of forts in 1867.

In 1872, the fort reverted to Britain and the name Metalen Kruis was Anglicised as Metal Cross.

Thereafter, the fort was used as District

Officers' residence and offices, State Council, police and post offices ■

Above left: before restoration, the tower was made of wood
Above right: numerous embrasures and heavy canons kept approaches to the fort under guard.
Right: the fort is nowadays a rest house with a beautiful view of the fishing harbour.

GROSS-FRIEDRICHSBURG - PRINCESTOWN

1683 BRANDENBURG   1717-24 AHANTA   1725 NETHERLANDS   1872 BRITAIN

Above : the fort c.1782
Right : the only German fort of Africa is now a comfortable rest house.

In 1682, a group of European financiers and ship owners led by Benjamin Raule established the Brandenburg Africa Company under the patronage of the Great Elector, Frederick William of Brandenburg. The company's objective was to break the trade monopoly of the Dutch West Indian Company in the Gold Coast.

In the Brandenburg-Ahanta agreement, the local chiefs and people were told : "You bound yourselves by oath to trade with no one whomsoever except our ships and people and to indicate to our officers a site whereon to build a fort and to accept us as your protector."

The agreement also enjoined the Brandenburgers to ensure that no local women or children were sold into slavery. The Ahanta chief of Pokesu, (later called Prinze Terre or Princes Town), allocated land on a promontory where, in 1683-84, the Brandenburg company built a major fort and named it Groot Friedrichsborg after Brandenburg's Great Elector, Frederick William.

The fort was located on Manfro hill, five kilometres east of Fort St. Anthony, Axim. It was a fairly large square fort with four bastions and thick parapets linked by wide curtain walls. It had a courtyard lined on three sides by two-storeyed buildings large enough to accommodate staff numbering over ninety. All units of the fort - residences, storage rooms and fortification - were exceptionally well-constructed and special imported bricks were used for pavements, vaulting and coigning.

Contemporary European visitors to Princes Town were singularly impressed by "the fort's big bell tower and most imposing and most beautiful gate of the entire coast" and Groot-Friedrichsburg was described as "one of the most luxurious forts on the coast." Although other trade forts were raised by Brandenburg at Takrama (1685) and Akwada (1687),

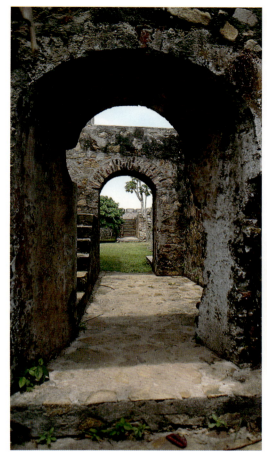

Above : the door of no return.
Centre : the main building outdoor staircase
Right : the main courtyard

Friedrichsburg became the headquarters of Brandenburg's possessions.
The Brandenburg Company's avowed objective was to establish its own monopoly in a district already partially occupied by Dutch and English forts. To ensure success, Brandenburg concentrated its efforts in the gold-rich Ahanta and Nzema region and also appointed as its "Broker", John Conny, an Ahanta chief noted for his trading and political shrewdness. Conny established links with hinterland

states like Wassa, Asante, Denkyira etc. to guarantee a constant supply of gold to Friedrichsburg. Besides, captains of English interloper ships preferred to trade at Friedrichsburg rather than at Cape Coast Castle. Historical records indicate that in two years, 1711-13, no less than 95 ships traded with Friedrichsburg. In 1716, the last Brandenburg Commandant left Princes Town. In 1717, Brandenburg declared its intention to sell its possessions to the Dutch but its ally Conny was not informed officially. Conny captured the fort and assumed the governorship. He accelerated trade with ship captains from all European nations, offering gold and slaves at "cut-throat prices", 20 percent below prices offered at other forts and castles.

According to the Dutch West Indian Company records at the Hague archives, in May 1718, Captain Van der Hoeven was ordered "to lead an expedition to acquire the fortress Great Friedrichsburg illegally taken in possession by Connie". The Axim populace declined to assist the Dutch. Three Dutch ships shelled Princes Town with fire balls, grenades and shots but without success. The Hague archives state : "One hundred and twenty well-

armed men landed to scale the fort but they met with heavy fire and in a few minutes most of them were dead. Van der Hoeven himself was also wounded but managed with a few other survivors to swim back to the boats."

This spectacular victory of Chief Conny over the Dutch army somehow reverberated around the African Diaspora and has been celebrated all over the black Caribbean since the late 18th century in the "John Canoe" Festivals. These involve street parades, costumed masquerades and dancing to the music of the fife-and-drum or goombay frame drum. Goombay drum-music was taken in 1800 by Jamaican freed slaves to Freetown, Sierra Leone, from where it spread all over West Africa and laid an important foundation for 20th century popular music styles such as Sierra Leonian maringa and ashiko, Ghanaian high life and Nigerian juju music.

In 1724, the Dutch succeeded eventually in dislodging John Conny and his Pokesu army from Fort Friedricksburg but not before Conny had despoiled it of many stones and other materials for use in constructing a mansion for himself.

Upon its capture, the fort was renamed Hollandia by the Dutch and reconstructed in parts. But the fort never regained its former glory ■

Above : the male slave prison.
Right : view of ocean sunset from the fort.

FORT ST. ANTHONY - AXIM

1515 PORTUGAL   1642 NETHERLANDS   1872 BRITAIN

Following the establishment of their headquarters at Elmina, the Portuguese, in an effort to maintain their monopoly and exclude foreign ships from the gold markets, built a trade post in 1503 at Axim close to the mouth of the River Ankobra. Owing to attacks launched by the local people on the lodge, the trade post was abandoned. In 1515, a small promontory close to the Ankobra mouth was chosen and a fort built to cover the entire promontory. It was named Santo Antonio and was the second Portuguese fort on the Gold Coast. The site chosen had several little inselbergs in the ocean close to the promontory.

The fort was triangular in outline, in keeping with the contours of the promontory. Two major bastions were located on the northern and southern ends - the two corners of the wide end of the triangle. They were linked by a curved battery. The Portuguese constructed a rock-cut ditch some three metres deep to protect the landward side of the fort but this was later filled in during the 17th century. Inside the fort, a number of buildings of considerable size were raised to accommodate up to thirty officers. After the fall of

Above : the fort c.1682
Right : seaward bastion canons
Next two pages : inner buildings, outside and inside.

Elmina Castle to the Dutch in 1637, Fort St. Antonio was able to hold out for four and a half years. This is a testimony to the strength of the Portuguese fortifications there. During the period of Portuguese monopoly, they opened a gold mine near Axim. The fact that beside St. Anthony there was no other trading post in the gold-rich lands of the Ankobra and Tano River valleys gave tremendous economic and strategic importance to the fort. In fact, gold traders from Adanse and Denkyira came regularly to Fort St. Anthony. On the other hand, during the period c.1650-1720, European competition for bases and trade increased and forts were built in the bays east of Axim. Trade wars became rampant with Africans allying themselves to rival European nations. Under the circumstances, the Dutch embarked on a major period of fort construction and reconstruction : Three-storied buildings were raised inside the fort for use as residences, offices and store rooms. Also, a service yard and outworks were constructed.

After the 1720's with the dissolution of the Brandenburg Company and the death of its principal ally, John Conny, inter-European hostile competition in the area abated and Dutch trade increased. By 1706 it was reported that the Dutch were able to amass "more gold at Axim than anywhere else together." Moreover, the Axim area became an important source of supply of timber for Dutch forts and in the 18th century, the Dutch established cotton plantations there.

In 1872, Fort St. Anthony was ceded to Britain. It was rehabilitated in the 1950's and its rooms have since been used as government and local council offices ■

Left : aerial view
Right : Fort St Anthony overlooking an Axim bay sunrise.

FORT APOLLONIA - BEYIN

1768 BRITAIN   1868 NETHERLANDS

The coastlands west of the mouth of the River Ankobra are characterised by a long sandy beach interrupted by lagoons and swamps. At Beyin, however, there is a stretch of flat solid sandy ground above the beach. The Tano basin and the Ankasa forest in the hinterlands of Beyin are rich in gold and timber. Thus, even though the coastlands were unsuitable for fort-building and harbours, European nations, especially the French, Dutch and English competed for a foothold in the area. The English Committee of Merchants, in response to an invitation from the Nzema Chief Amenihyia, built the last English fort above the beach at Beyin. The English employed slave labour and quarried limestone rock from a nearby site to build the fort in 1768-70.

The name Apollonia, chosen for the fort, was first conferred on the area by the Portuguese explorer who sighted the place on St. Apollonia's day. Shortly after the abolition of the slave trade, gradual economic decline set in and the English abandoned the fort in 1819. In 1868, Fort Apollonia was transferred to the Dutch who renamed it after their monarch, Willem III, and held it till 1872.

Above and right : the fort was completely restored in the 1960's as a rest house.
Left : the main entrance leading to the courtyard.
Below : canon ornating the main entrance.

maritime enemy attack and also because it was hollowed for use as a slave prison. The other three bastions were smaller and designed to carry up to five guns.

The fort was severely damaged in 1873 when a British gunboat bombarded Beyin on account of its alliance with the Asante kingdom. The fort fell into ruins but was rehabilitated in the 1960's by the Ghana Museums and Monuments Board and has since been used as a rest house ∎

Right : Latest of the small forts built by the English in tropical Africa, Apollonia consists, unlike any other on the Coast, almost wholly of limestone.

Architecturally, the fort is irregular in plan and square in outline with four bastions linked by curtain walls. The bastions are of different shape and size : The west bastion was strategically given a disproportionately large size and extra solidity and had nine mounted guns because of its exposure to

CONCLUSION

The gates of return
Bibliography
Aknowledgments

THE GATES OF RETURN

The saga of European fort-building on the Gold Coast spans three centuries from 1482 to 1787. Although several trade posts have fallen into a state of decay or have totally disappeared, many others have been conserved and adapted to new usages and so continue to be maintained.

As the castles and forts have been elevated by UNESCO to the status of World Heritage Monuments that must of necessity be preserved for posterity and for world cultural development, it seems appropriate to reflect on them once again and to visualise them through the eyes of their original European makers and their African partners as well as those of living Africans and the Black Diaspora today.

As indicated earlier, the original purpose of the construction of the European forts was to protect their occupants and their business enterprises from the attentions of hostile European rivals and African intruders and enemies. For their part, the local chiefs and elders regarded the fort and factories essentially as revenue-paying units. The Europeans were obliged to pay annual ground rent and various "taxes" and "gifts" on a regular basis. For instance, in 1650, the Swedish African Company paid 323,712 dambas in gold to the chief of Afutu as rent for the company's fort. In 1659-72, the Danish Company paid over 2 million dambas in gold to the Accra and Afutu chiefs for their three trading stations. Also, it was expected that in return for the territory leased to the European Company for building the fort, the fort's garrison and guns would come to the aid of the African settlement whenever it was attacked by a hostile force. Essentially this was expected to be a partnership of positive symbiosis. Unfortunately, in several cases, individual selfish interests held sway and neither Europeans nor their African partners could be trusted to respect the terms of the land contracts.
In a dispatch to his superiors in the Netherlands, in 1717 the director-general of Elmina Castle, Engelgraaf Robbertsz, expressed dissatisfaction with the fickleness of the African partners in settlements at Commany, Sekondi, Cormantin, Butre, Mouri and Accra. The Dutch debated whether or not some non-viable forts should be closed down :

"The natives have founded special croms under each fort, depending on the profit they expect from either us or the English and each has its Caboceer who maintains with other natives in the interior and who brings these, to whom he feels most inclined, to the forts to sell their gold, slaves and tusks. If we were to abandon such forts, it would be regarded as a sign of impotence of the company and those under our protection would join the remaining nation. The English would also regard this as an opportunity to make themselves masters of the entire coast and its trade because we have often seen that all our contracts and agreements with the Africans hold only as long as they see advantage in them. The Fantyn natives at Cormantyn would not allow us to go because of their annual claim of ships gifts. Long experience has taught us that the Negroes are by nature slavish and that they want nothing but to submit themselves to a mighty yoke and to serve only those who have the power to put loads on their backs and spurs into their sides."

The reasons for this situation in the early 18th century in which a policy of mutual mistrust seemed to be the order of the day appears to be that :
1) Originally, in the 15th and 16th centuries, the African-European relationship was viewed as a partnership solely between Portuguese Europeans and some particular coastal African states for mutual benefit through monopolistic trade.
2) Over the decades, as a large number of rival official European companies as well as private European companies (including the numerous "ten percenters") entered the coastal trade, the coast increasingly crystallized into a "frontier of opportunity ". By the middle to late 17th century the coastal society had assumed the character of a "middleman" society sandwiched between the Europeans on the coast and the hinterland African states such as Denkyira, Wassa, Aowin, Sefwi, Akyem, Adanse etc. The coastal "middleman" societies gradually developed, it seems, an insatiable taste for "consumerism".
3) However, the coastal African societies also depended on the hinterland states, (in whose lands the bulk of the gold deposits were actually located), to provide the gold that facilitated exchange for imported European goods. As more and more gold was exchanged for material wealth (that could be built into capital) and military hardware, as the hinterland states equipped themselves militarily and economically and also developed a taste for "consumerism" there was bound to be a confrontation between the African hinterland and the coastal Africans and their European allies. This was the situation by the early 18th century when Asante emerged as a powerful hinterland state.

What was the nature of the apparently "consumerist" middleman coastal African society ? From well-documented European sources, there were three major classes of people among the coastal Akan : upper class, commoners and slaves.
The Upper Class was comprised of; nobility (afahene, awuranom), politico-military stalwarts (ahenfo, abrafo), mercantile group (abirempon, batafo), priests-ideologists (asafo, abosomfo, asumanfo).
This group engrossed public, political and socioeconomic power. It was of "noble birth" or had acquired a nobility status. It alone could buy, own and sell slaves, retainers and bonded commoners. An Afahene had slaves, servants and retainers engaged in some twenty different services and functions at his beck and call. As Jean Barbot noted in the 17th century "slaves are one part of the Afahene's riches and property, a commodity in this country." The authority of the Abirempon seemed limitless : they had the know-how of trade-routes, caravans, commercial transactions, movements of goods, prices of goods, lingua franca ; they mediated in disputes, drew up treaties and agreements etc.
They had large mansions, very expensive clothing, costly jewellery and enjoyed varieties of imported food. On the other hand, the commoners or lower class (Anihumanifo, Adofo, Adwumafo) had relatively few material possessions. Yet they served as the artisans, farmers, traders, military men, labourers, fishermen, shiploaders and canoe men. Thirdly, there were the slaves, who were bonded to the upper class.

By the mid-17th century, the gold trade was giving way to the slave trade. Dutch West-Indian Company Director Rademacher wrote in February 1730 to Holland: "The Gold Coast has now virtually changed into a pure Slave Coast. The great quantity of guns and gunpowder which the Europeans have brought there has given cause to terrible wars among the kings, princes and caboceers of those lands who made their prisoners of war slaves. These slaves are bought at steadily increasing prices. Consequently, there is now very little trade among the coast Negroes except in slaves. The English send every year hundreds of ships and the French, Danes and Portuguese send many too."

During the 18th century peak period of the Atlantic trade the figures for Gold Coast export of slaves were;
1700-1740........230,000
1741-1770........220,000
1771-1800........227,000
Total................677,000

It is estimated that the male-female ratio of the slave exports from West Africa was 51,3% for males and 48,7% for females. Moreover the slaves exported were largely those in the age bracket 16-30 years. This means that the majority of the slaves exported were those who were in the reproductive age-groups.

Thus the export slave trade had a depressing effect on birth rates during the period that it lasted.

In centuries and decades past, many scholars and non-scholars alike have tried to apportion blame for the atrocities and evils of the slave trade, one way or the other. It may be argued that the Europeans constituted the "senior partner" in the African-European partnership in terms of the apparent superiority they had in know-how, possession of material culture, goods and technology. Thus the attitudes and behaviour patterns of the "senior partner" were emulated by the "junior partner".

This issue came up when the law abolishing the slave trade was passed. No less than two important kings of West Africa protested against unilateral abolition.

In the 1720's, Whydah became Dahomey's major port of trade. Records show that by the 1750's, it alone was exporting more slaves than all the trading stations of the Gold Coast put together. The King of Dahomey remarked to Governor Abson of the African Company's fort at Whydah: "What hurts me most is that some of your people have maliciously represented us in books that never die, alleging that we sell our wives and children for the sake of a few kegs of brandy. No. We are shamefully belied. Tell posterity that we have been abused. We do indeed sell to the white men a part of our prisoners and we have a right so to do. Are not all prisoners at the disposal of their captors? And are we to blame if we send delinquents to a far country? I have been told you do the same!"
(A. Dalzel: *The History of Dahomey*. London. 1793, p. 219)

In another dialogue with Joseph Dupuis, British Consul at Kumasi, the Asantehene Osei Bonsu stated:

"The white men do not understand my country or they would not say the slave trade was bad. But if they think it bad now, why did they think it good before? Is not your law an old law, the same as the Crammo (Moslem) law? Crammos say the law is good because the great God made the book, so they buy slaves. You must put down in my master's book all I shall say and then he will look to it

now he is my friend. And when he sees what is true, he will surely restore that trade. I cannot make war to catch slaves in the bush, like a thief. My ancestors never did so. But if I fight a king and kill him when he is insolent, then certainly I must have his gold and his slaves and the people are mine too. Do not the white kings act like this?"
(J. Dupuis, *Journal of a Residence in Ashantee*, London 1824).

However negative the slave trade may have been, through its instrumentality the native African cultural traditions were transplanted to the New World. For instance, wherever slaves of Akan origin had the opportunity, they revived the Akan cultures of Ghana. The maroons or "Bush Negroes" of Surinam, the maroons of Haiti, Jamaica, Santo Domingo, South Georgia and the Gulla Islands provide illustrations of transplanted Akan culture in the New World. Among the Bush Negroes of Dutch and French Guiana, we find Fante-Asante Ghanaian culture in its purest form, in terms of language, art, folk lore, masks, religion, instruction, social organization, economic life and technology.

The naming custom using the list of "day-names" as applicable among the Akan of Ghana is exactly paralleled in the Guianas. They name their people "Conachi, Codio, Couamina, Couacou, Yao, Cofi, Couami".

Among the Gullahs of Carolina, the 18th century African slaves were named by the Akan system. In Jamaica there is worship of Akan Onyame; the "ancestors" are venerated, and the Cormantin cult worship has been practised for generations. Miss Nancy, the trickster featured in Jamaican folktales, is none other than the shrewd trickster Kweku Ananse of Akan folkloric narratives.

Many African American forms of dance such as the Charleston show influence from the Akwasidae festival of Asante. In St. Lucia, the Akan yam festival has been observed annually among the Negroes and, in Barbados, Asante funeral customs have been observed in recent times.

Such is the legacy of the African-European relationships established on the Gold Coast as these two peoples met at the castles, forts and lodges between 1482-1880.

If the castles and forts gangways leading to the slave ships once appeared to be "the doors of no return", thanks to the new spirit of reconciliation and the UNESCO institutionalisation of the Castle and Fort culture, now it has become "a new Akwaaba" for the black Diaspora, the "Gates of Return" into their second home, their real home, in Africa! ∎

Next double page:
the Gates of Return at Dixcove Fort

ANNEX

BIBLIOGRAPHY

AKYEAMPONG E. 1996. *Drink, Power and Culture Change*. James Currey. London.

ANQUANDAH K.J. 1982. *Rediscovering Ghana's Past*. Longman. London.

ADLER P. BARNARD N. 1992. *Asafo!* Thames and Hudson. London

ASIMENG M. 1981. *The Social Structure of Ghana*. Ghana Publishing Corp. Tema.

BAETA C.G. 1962. *Prophetism in Ghana*. SCMP Press, London.

BAME K.N.1994. *Come to Laugh, African Traditional Theatre in Ghana*. Lilian Barber Press. New York.

BARBER K. COLLINS E.J. and RICARD A.1997. *West African Popular Theatre*. Indiana University Press.

BARBOT J. 1732. *A Description of the Coasts of North and South Guinea*. Paris.

BEECHAM J. 1824. *Ashanti and the Gold Coast*. John Mason. London.

BILBY K.M. 1985. *The Caribbean as a Musical Region*. The Woodrow Wilson International Centre for Scholars. Washington DC.

BIRMINGHAM W. NEUSTADT J. and OMABOE E.M. 1967. *A Study of Contemporary Ghana*. George, Allen and Unwin. London.

BOSMAN W. 1705. *New and Accurate Description of the Coast of Guinea*. J. Krapton. London.

BOWDICH T. 1819. *Mission to Cape Coast and Ashantee*. John Murray. London.

CARMICHAEL J. 1993. *African Eldorado*. Duckworth. London.

COLLINS E.F. 1962. *The Panic Element in 19th Century British Relations with Ashanti*. In : Transactions of the Historical Society of Ghana. Vol V, Part 2, University of Ghana, pp 79-144. Legon.

COLLINS E.J. 1985. *Music Makers of West Africa*. Three Continents Press Washington DC and Lynne Rienner Publications, Boulder, Colorado.

COLLINS E.J. 1994.1996. *Highlife Time*. Anansesem Press. Accra.

COLLINS E.J. 1996. *E.T. Mensah the King of Highlife*. Anansesem Press. Accra.

DICKSON K.B. 1969. *A Historical Geography of Ghana*. Oxford University Press.

DUPUIS J. 1824. *Journal of a Residence in Asante*. Henri Colburn. London.

FIELD M. 1937. *Religion and Medicine Among the Ga People*. Oxford University Press.

FREEMAN R. 1898. *Travels and Life in Ashanti and Jaman*.

GARLICK P.C. 1971. *African Traders and Economic Development in Ghana*. Clarendon Press, Oxford.

DE GRAFT JOHNSON J.C. 1932. *The Fanti Asafu. In : The Journal of the Institute of African Languages and Culture*. D. Westerman. Oxford University Press. Vol V. PP 307-322

HILL P. 1963. *The Migrant Cocoa Farmer of Southern Ghana*. Cambridge University Press.

KEA R. 1982. *Settlements, Trade and Polities in the 17th Century Gold Coast*. John Hopkins University. London.

LAWRENCE. A.W. 1963. *Trade Castles and Forts of West Africa*. Jonathan Cape. London.

LITTLE K. 1970. *West African Urbanisation*. Cambridge University Press.

NKETIA J.H.K. 1963. *Drumming in Akan Communities*. University of Ghana and Thomas Nelson and Sons. London.

NKETIA J.H.K. 1974. *Music of Africa*. W.W.

Norton. New York.

OPOKU K.A. 1978. *West African Traditional Religion*. FEP International Private Ltd. Singapore and Accra.

PRIEBE R.K. 1988. *Ghanaian Literatures*. Greenwood Press Westport. Connecticut.

RATTRAY R. S 1923. *Ashanti*. Clarendon Press. Oxford.

RATTRAY R.S. 1929. *Ashanti Law and Constitution*. Clarendon Press. Oxford.

ROBERTS J.S. 1974. *Black Music of Two Worlds*. William Morrow and Company. New York.

SUTHERLAND E. 1970. *The Original Bob*. Anawuo Educational Publications. Accra.

SECRETAN T. 1995. *Fantastic Coffins of Ghana*. Thames and Hudson. London.

TWUMASI P.A. 1975. *Medical Systems of Ghana*. Ghana Publishing Corporation. Tema.

WARD W.E. 1927. *Music in The Gold Coast*. Gold Coast Review. Vol. 3. N°2. Accra.

WARD W.E. 1948. *A History of Ghana*. George Allen and Unwin. London.

WILKS I. 1979. *Asante in the 19th century*. Cambridge University Press.

KWESI J. ANQUANDAH

61, BA (History) ; Dip. Archeology ; M. Litt. (Oxford) is a professor of Archeology at the University of Ghana and a member of the Ghana Monuments and Museums Board. Author of several books, numerous monographs and studies illuminating his country's archeological and historical patrimony, Prof. Anquandah is popular in Ghana for over 250 radio programmes like "Them and Now", "Ghana's Cultural Heritage," "African Landmarks" which helped his fellow countrymen to measure the depth and scope of their past history. Since the early 1990's, he has conducted a programme of archeological excavations in the Castles of Elmina and Cape Coast and contributes to the development of both Museums.

THIERRY SECRETAN

43, has been a free lance writer, photographer and film maker in Africa since 1979. His articles and photos have been published in *The New-York Times Magazine*, *Stern*, *Le Monde*, *The Observer*, *Paris Match*, *The Washington Post*, *Le Figaro*, *Geo*, *El País*, etc. His documentary films have been broadcast in prime time by the *BBC*, *CBS*, *National Geographic Explorer*, *NHK*, *Canal+*, *France 2*, *ARTE* etc. Four of these documentaries were dedicated to Ghana. His book, "Going into darkness" (Il fait sombre va-t'en. Hazan) on the customized coffins of Ghana, the first on the subject, was published in 1994 in Paris by Hazan and in 1995 by Thames and Hudson in the United Kingdom and the USA.

ACKNOWLEDGMENTS

This book was made possible thanks to the initiative of H. E the President of the Republic of Ghana Flt Lt Jerry John Rawlings and the First Lady, H. E Nana Konadu Agyeman Rawlings.

The authors wish also to thank the Ghana Museums and Monuments Board for its confidence as well as the Ghana Air Force and the personnel of the various administrations they contacted who invariably proved to be enthusiastic about this project, particularly;

Mr Kwame Peprah
Nii Okaija Adamafio
Mr Kofi Totobi Quakyi
Nana Ato Dadzie
Ms Valerie Sackey
Mr. Harry O. Blavo
Dr Ben Abdalah
Mr Kobina Wudu
Dr Isaac K. Debrah
Mr James Ampadu
Mr Kwesi Opoku Acheampong
Takoradi Harbour Authority
Georges Padmore Library
Group Cpt Kwame Mamphey
Wing Commander Augustus Lawson
Flt Lt Samuel Abrokwa
Chief Super Intendent Nordor
Mr Fritz Baffour
Ms Erika Wilson
Dr John Collins
Ms Doris Quansah
Mr John Carmichael
Ms Elisabeth Kamara
Mr Ramses Cleland
Mr Joe Nkrumah
Mr Georges Olympio
Ms Julie Glover
Dr Joe Gazari Seini
Ms Susan Anquandah
Ms Régine Secretan
Mr Peter Adler
Mr Andrew Biney
Ms Augusta Conchiglia
Mr Theo Hakola
Mr Subi Kalmoni
Mr Steven Korsah
Mr Bob Nater
Mr Michel Folco
Mr Pierre-Yves Sachet
Mr Kingsley Yeboah

Castles & Forts of Ghana
is a Ghana Museums & Monuments Board's book.
Barnes Road P. O. Box 3343 Accra, Ghana

This edition © 1999 Atalante / Paris
42 rue Sedaine, 75011 Paris, France
E-mail atalant@calva. net

© Kwesi J. Anquandah for the text
© all photographs by Thierry Secretan
except p. 17 (courtesy P. Adler/T & Hudson)

Printed in Belgium

ISBN 2-9513901-0-6